Author's note: The following story is a work of fiction. All statements attributed to Ayn Rand are based upon my interpretation of her published works, and may or may not conform to her actual beliefs or what her actual reaction to the events in the story would have been. I leave it to you, the reader, to make that determination.

Being retired, I have a lot of time on my hands. I spend many of my days just walking the side streets of New York City, seeing whatever there is to see that day. There are the second hand stores, the pawn shops, book stores and tourist traps that offer their wares. I seldom buy anything due to my limited income, but once in a while something catches my eyes. That's what happened when I passed a particularly dusty pawn shop window this morning. Through its grimy windows I saw something I hadn't seen for years, an old typewriter. It looked like one from a 1940's movie newsroom. I could just barley make out the faded manufactures name, Remington Rand. That was the kind that I had learned to type on some sixty years ago, when I was ten or eleven years old. Curious, I went inside to get a better look at it. The proprietor took it out of the window and dusted it off. He looked at a tag on it and said I could have it for ten dollars, case included. I noticed that the date on the tag was 1982. He handed me a blank sheet of paper, which I rolled into the machine, and started typing, "Now is the time for all good men to come to the aid of their country". The ribbon was quite faded, but the keys worked well enough. I asked him if he knew who the previous owner was.

He pulled a dusty book off of a shelf and leafed through it. "I always make notes about my purchases in case I've sold it before they come back. It was dropped off by some young guy who said it had belonged to a famous author that had died. He wanted an extra twenty because of that. I didn't give it to him of course. I'm not in the souvenir business. He assured me he'd come back for it, because it meant a lot to him, but he never did. What with computers and word processors, nobody uses them anymore. What would you do with it?"

"I'm sort of an antique collector. I like old things. I have a radio from the 1930's and an old black and white TV from the 1950's. I used to be an electronics engineer and it sort of a hobby of mine to keep that old stuff working. Don't know what I'll do with this, but it's only ten bucks, so I'll take it."

I put it in its case and gave him the money. When I got home I set the case aside and went to log on to my computer, an old Apple IIe. I had bought it when they first came out in the 1980's, and had added various upgrades as they had become available. I had written some programs of my own and installed them, and it was now a unique computer, like no other in the world. I don't even remember how some of the programs work anymore.

I logged onto the internet to catch up on the news and find out what was the latest disaster battering the country. The economy was bad and getting worse. The government had already bailed out auto manufactures, banks and insurance companies. The public wanted their bad mortgages re-written and credit card debts forgiven. The International Money Fund wanted us to give it billions of dollars to bail out the PIIGS countries. Congress had nationalized health care and passed new laws to control "Wall Street" and now planned to pass something they called "cap and trade". There was a disastrous oil spill in the Gulf of Mexico. We seemed to go from one crisis to another with barely enough time to catch our breath. Government was getting bigger and bigger, and talk of Socialism was everywhere. We've come a long way from the "can do" spirit of the Reagan years. What a difference one generation can make. It was very discouraging.

I logged off of the news and went to a game zone and started doing a crossword puzzle. There was no point in dwelling on politics, there wasn't anything that I could do about it. As I started filling in the puzzle, I noticed that my keyboard was sticking. Being about twenty five years old, it had seen better days. It was time to shop the pawnshops for another one. I logged off and shut down the computer. I picked up the typewriter and set it on my kitchen table. Using the small brush on my vacuum cleaner I gave it a thorough cleaning, lubricated the keys and shift levers, then put a piece of paper in and typed a few words. It had a nice feel to it, much better then a stiff computer keyboard. Too bad they couldn't make them as good as these old typewriters. It would probably cost a fortune to do it with all those metal keys. Then the idea came to me, why not hook up the typewriter keyboard to the computer? It would take some work, but it could be done. What a challenge it would be, and if I succeeded I would surely have the most unique computer in the world.

It took weeks to hunt down all the parts that I needed. Some could only be found on the internet. I had to rework many of them to make them compatible with my computer, but that was part of the fun. When I was finally finished I opened my word processor and gave it a try.

"Now is the time for all good men to come to the aid of their country" I typed and saw the words appear on the monitor. . It worked perfectly. I sat back in by chair and glowed with self-satisfaction. Then, to my astonishment, more words began to appear on the screen.

"So why are you just sitting there letting your country goes to hell?"

I rubbed my eyes, but the question remained. "This is it!" I thought, "I'm going senile." I sat there, staring at the computer screen. More words began to form. "Why don't you answer me?" I sat frozen with panic. More words appeared. "Who are you?"

This isn't possible, I thought. Words can't appear without pressing keys on the keyboard. The computer can't create words to say to me.

More words appeared on my monitor: "DAMN YOU, WHY DON'T YOU ANSWER ME!"

Then it occurred to me that this must be some sort of scam, somebody must have hacked into my computer. All right, I thought, I'll go ahead with this game and see where it leads. I started typing, "My name is John Stewart, who are you?"

"Who am I? You ask 'who am I?' to one of the most famous writers that ever lived? You use my typewriter, the one that I wrote 'The Fountainhead' and 'Atlas Shrugged' on, and you ask 'Who am I'?"

I had read those books in college, so I knew immediately who the writer claimed to be. But that was impossible of course. I started typing, "Ayn Rand is dead, and therefore you couldn't be her, unless you're a ghost. Are you?"

"Don't be a fool, there's no such thing as ghosts. The typewriter you are using was a part of my life for ten to fifteen hours a day, sometimes more, seven days a week for more than forty years. My spirit is as much a part of it as the keys that you press. Now, somehow, I find myself able to write without touching the keys. It is a new and invigorating experience. I have somehow become integrated with your computer's circuitry. I can even access the internet. The flow of information is incredible, if only I had been able to do this while I was alive. Of course the bad new is that my beloved adopted country, America, is destroying itself just as I predicted that it would. I wish that I had been wrong about that. It's people like you that let it happen."

That made me angry. "Me?" I typed. "Why do you blame me? I voted for every conservative politician that ever ran for office. I tried to persuade my friends to do the same. I spoke out for conservative causes. What more could I have done?"

"Conservatives! Don't get me started on them. Look at the one that just left the White House. He socialized prescription medicine and bailed out the banks. The so called 'conservative' Republican opposition to this is not, 'He is using taxpayer money to support failing companies, which is immoral, and central planning is destructive and un-American.' No, its 'There is no guarantee that it will succeed'. Just what do you suppose was being conserved?"

"He's was trying to save our economy."

"He's was destroying it. Government intervention in the markets caused this crisis, so how can more of it end it? First your government passed the Community Reinvestment Act, which forced banks to make risky loans to people that couldn't afford them. The government then applied pressure to Fannie Mae and Freddie Mac to buy and guarantee those loans, making them seem safer than they actually were. All of this was happening while the Federal Reserve was keeping interest rates artificially low, causing a housing bubble. These very risky loans were then packaged as 'derivatives' and resold to companies like AIG. Finally, the government had to bail out the companies that bought these investments when they turned out to be worthless. AIG got $150 billion, and $200 billion went to Fannie Mae and Freddie Mac, to start with. It's just one more example of government trying to perform a 'noble' service, and leaving a path of destruction in its wake. The private companies should have been allowed to fail. 'Creative destruction' is an intrinsic part of Capitalism. Like dead branches on a tree, failed companies must be pruned so that new growth can occur."

"That's not practical; there would have been panic in the streets."

"That might happen anyway, look at what's happening in Greece."

"You seem to know a lot about what's happening today for someone that died more than twenty five years ago."

"I told you, I have instantaneous access to the internet. I have the joy of infinite information and the sorrow of knowing what it all means. America today is like the tree on the Taggart family estate, a vast, imposing structure on the outside but a hollowed out, rotting shell internally."

"Then you must realize that in the real world people don't act like the heroes in your novels. Instead of Howard Roarks and Hank Reardens we have people like Angelo Mozilo, who headed Countrywide and was paid $100 million as he destroyed the company. While he was raking in the cash 120,000 of his home loans were in foreclosure. The people at Fanny Mea, Freddy Mac and AGI, were no better. All of these people took the money and ran, like thieves in the night. How do you explain that?"

"But don't you see, Daniel Mudd, who was CEO of Fannie Mae, is the personification of my character Orren Boyle. He worked for a company charted by congress and received enormous salaries while he destroyed the company. It lost $2.1 billion in 2007 while the value of its shares dropped 33%. For this performance he received total compensation of almost thirteen million dollars!

"In my novels I show the Statists, such as Mr. Mudd, as they actually are and my heroes as they could be. The Statists want to control every aspect of you life, including how you live and when you die. As you noted, those people are like thieves. They create nothing of value but demand the right to confiscate what value you create and distribute it as they please. Then they claim the right to tell you how to spend what little you have left."

"So you still think that government intervention is the main threat to our country?"

"Yes, combined with the so called 'green movement,' which it fully supports."

"How can an effort to save the planet's environment be a threat?"

"Mankind advances by shaping nature to its needs. By doing this you have pulled yourselves out of the caves and a minimal life expectancy consisting of an unending hunt for food. The environmentalist would have you return to a state of worshiping nature instead of using it, a state that leads back to the caves."

"Don't you think that's a bit excessive? Asking us to use more efficient light bulbs and refrigerators is not putting us on a path to living like cavemen."

"Philosophically, it is. It puts you on a path to the dark ages before the age of reason. It states that the size of your environmental 'footprint' is a measure of your guilt! Like the concept of 'original sin,' its aim is to make you feel guilty for being alive, and nothing that you can do can remove that guilt. You have 'philosophers' that state that the end of human life on earth should be greeted with a 'good riddance' and biologist that state that human happiness is not as important as a wild and healthy planet. Your scientists distort evidence about global warming and then call it 'settled science'. They claim that industrialization is causing the warming, ignoring the fact that there is evidence that temperatures might have been warmer during the medieval ages than they are today. The best thing that you can do for their movement is to die, and therefore stop using the earth's resources and the government's finances. That's why they included in the government health insurance plan a provision stating that the elderly be instructed on ways to commit suicide. Stated simply, they worship death instead of life!

"What has happened in America since the inauguration of President Obama is an acceleration of everything I wrote about in 'Atlas Shrugged'. He has managed to accomplish in little over a year what I envisioned would take more than a decade! Consider the most basic threats to Capitalism in America today: Over-taxation; government controlled health care; cap-and-trade legislation; Supreme Court Judges making laws; vast government bureaucracies; Government run education; uncontrolled immigration; runaway entitlements; and an insane foreign policy based upon weakness and supplication. All of these are contrary to the intent of your Constitution, yet they are allowed to exist. Your government has nothing but contempt for its citizens. This was illustrated by your President when he talked about people 'clinging desperately to their guns and Bibles', and again by the Speaker of the house when she referred to citizens critical of her health care plan as 'astro-turf'. The most liberal and elitist Supreme Court Justice ever, Thurgood Marshall, said that the Constitution '...was defective from the start...' His way of correcting those defects, as he explained to his law clerk, was 'You do what you think is right and let the law catch up.' In other words, 'I'll ignore the Constitution and make my own laws', which is exactly what he did. There, in their own words, you hear what the highest level of leadership in each branch of your government thinks about the Constitution and the people they have been elected to serve."

"I'm not sure I understand the connection between "Atlas Shrugged" and what's happening in the country today."

"Then let me give you just one example, taxation. One of the themes of my novel is government's treatment of the producers of wealth in order to redistribute their wealth. That is happening today and has placed America's economy on a downward spiral and is creating class warfare. There is ample proof of this. In 2005 half of the income tax returns filed accounted for 97% of the taxes paid. The top 10% of earners paid 70% of them. Soon, more people will be receiving government services than are paying for them. The people supporting these free-loaders should and will rebel against this system."

"It is well established that lower tax rates lead to growing economies and reduced unemployment. The income tax cuts of the 1920's, from a top rate of 77% to just 29% in 1929 led to a sustained period of growth. From 1922 to 1929 the GNP grew at an average rate of 4.7% and unemployment fell from 6.7% to 3.2%. In the 1980's similar results occurred under the Reagan tax cuts. What is the current administration's plan to save your collapsing economy? They intend to do just the opposite, as Roosevelt did. Their results will be similar, a recession turned into a depression, a manufactured crisis. You will see a shrinking GNP and higher unemployment. They will blame this on the producers. After doing everything in their power to strangle production and remove any incentive to produce, they will criticize them for failing to produce!

"Think about the trial balloons now being sent up for a value added tax, a tax to be paid in addition to all of the already existing taxes. A tax on VALUE! A tax to be paid only by those that produce something! A lazy bum or incompetent wont pay that tax, the people that provide their sustenance will .It will be passed on to you, the consumer, every time that you buy your food, clothing, gasoline and other products that you require to live. This tax is common in the European Union, and look at the results. Five countries are on the verge of economic collapse, and they are already rioting and killing each other in one of them. The rates they talk about ranges from 15 to twenty five percent, to begin with. Let's assume 20 percent. Consider the average taxpayer in New York City. In addition to that he will pay a 15 percent Federal income tax, 7 percent state income tax, 3.5 percent city income tax, 9 percent state sales tax, 7 percent social security and medicare taxes, plus all of the hidden excise taxes. More that 63 percent of what he earns will be forcibly confiscated from him.

"Taxation is but one example. I know from your face book page that you are a retired electrical engineer. That is a profession that requires logic and reason. I shall therefore present other facts to you and let you form your own judgment. I believe that when I am finished you will agree that what is happening in America today is in accordance with the main theme of my novel, that there is a determined, well coordinated effort, at the highest level of your government, to impose Socialism on this country. Their justification for this will be, 'We have to consider the welfare of the common man and protect him from big corporations.' They are organizing the 'non-producers,' who are the recipients of their redistributions, to accomplish this goal. But America truly is exceptional, which your President refuses to acknowledge. Unlike Western Europe, your attitudes have never been compatible with an enormous government controlling your lives. Imposing their brand of socialism on America would be disastrous. But that is what the Statist are determined to do, as I shall prove to you. I will require some time to search the internet and prepare my presentation."

"All right, I'm going to attend a tea party rally in Central Park. I've never been to one, and I'm curious to see what they're all about. I'll get back to you afterwards. Will you be all right if I turn the computer off?"

"Yes, I'll be able to communicate with you as long as my typewriter remains connected to your computer. If it isn't, I'll be exploring the internet. It's an exhilarating experience; virtually everything known to man is there, waiting to be discovered"

I turned off the computer and put a dust cover over it and the typewriter, then I went outside and caught a bus to Central Park. When I got there the rally was already in progress, and the keynote speaker was addressing the thousands of people gathered there.

"…and our goal is a contract from America that any congressional candidates seeking our support must sign on to. What that contract requires is for these individuals to pledge to support our agenda to return our government to the principles of individual liberty, limited government and economic freedom."

He continued speaking, enumerating the ten points of the contract and what they were intended to accomplish. It was a comprehensive agenda, one that would send shock waves thru the country if it were passed. Point 4 called for a single-rate tax system to replace the current one. Point 6 wanted to limit the growth of federal spending. Point 7 wanted to repeal the Obama health care plan. Was this in fact the beginning of the class warfare that Ayn Rand had mentioned, the rebellion of the payers against the recipients of the benefits they paid for? I was curious to hear what else she had to say about the situation. I caught the next bus home and went to my computer.

I typed, "I'm back, are you ready to continue our discussion?"

"Yes, in order to allow for direct comparisons to "Atlas Shrugged" I shall utilize some prominent people to make comparisons to characters in my novel.

George Soros as Wesley Mouch
Jeffery Immelt , CEO of General Electric, as James Taggart
Al Gore, global warming crusader, as Dr. Floyd Ferris
Michael Mann, global warming scientist, as Dr. Simon Prichett
Keith Olbermann, news commentator, as Bertrund Scudder
Michael Moore, presumed intellectual, as Balf Eubank
Sara Palain, former governor of Alaska, as Dagny Taggart
Steve Jobs, entrepreneur, as Hank Rearden
President Obama as Mr. Thompson

"I will illustrate how each of the people listed above relates to the corresponding character in my novel, and the impact that they are having on your country today. I'll begin with Mr. Soros. In my novel Wesley Mouch is the major player in government, the man pulling the strings of power. He is a man that started his career selling bogus cure-all medicine. Mr. Soros is the major player on the political scene today. His money played a large role in the election of the President and gave the Liberals a majority in congress. How did he make his money, was it by creating products or services that people wanted to buy? No. It was by manipulating money markets and forcing England to devalue the Pound. This is the major financier of Statism.

His Open Society Institute contributed tens of millions of dollars to its causes, especially ACORN. Let me name some of the goals of the foundations receiving his funds: establishing the idea that we are an oppressive nation; opposing national security measures; promoting open borders and amnesty; promoting the expansion of welfare programs; advocating America's unilateral disarmament; promoting socialized medicine; promoting radical environmentalism; putting our foreign policy under the United Nations control; promoting racial and ethnic preferences. Like Wesly Mouch, he started out as an unknown, obscure individual. He used his money to obtain political connections that give him a voice in virtually every important decision being made by your government today, decisions that attack individualism and re-enforce collectivism. His plan for America is to make it into a European Union type of socialized country, with elites such as himself making decisions about how it is run."

As I thought about it, I had to agree that everything Mr. Soros supported was in line with the philosophy of the Wesley Mouch Character. But that didn't prove that there was an organized agenda to impose socialism on this country.

"What you say is true," I typed, "but that's only one man throwing his weight around. He can't socialize America all by himself."

"I agree, but he is not acting alone. I shall now introduce Mr. Immelt. James Taggart is the CEO of a large national corporation; Mr. Immelt is the CEO of a large multi-national corporation. Taggert became the head of his corporation when it was at its peak and ran it into the ground by wheeling and dealing with the government for special favors instead of using his abilities. He claimed to have had its most profitable year as it was on the verge of collapse. Immelt took over when G.E.'s stock price was 60, and it is now below 16. The company has lost many billions of dollars under his leadership. For this performance he received compensation of more than fourteen million dollars in 2007. But he has friends in high places in Washington. Despite being named one of the five worst CEOs of 2008, he was appointed to the President's Economic Recovery Advisory Board to provide advice and counsel! The fact that his company was fined fifty million dollars by the SEC in 2009 for breaking accounting rules and misleading investors didn't seem to bother the President. He is the perfect example of an incompetent CEO looking to the government to save his skin by awarding his company lucrative contracts."

I hadn't known about G.E.'s collapse. My savings are invested in mutual funds, and I don't follow the stock market very closely. I remember it as an appliance maker, with Ronald Reagan as its spokesman. Things certainly have changed.

"Let us look next at Al Gore, former career politician and present environmental crusader. Here is the ultimate 'insider', a man who was only a handful of votes away from becoming President, a Nobel peace prize winner and author of books about global warming. I shall quote a paragraph in my novel where Dr. Ferris is speaking. 'Now, you see...you are speaking as if this book were addressed to a thinking audience. If it were, one would have to be concerned with such matters as accuracy, validity, logic, and the prestige of science. But it isn't. It's addressed to the public.'

"Is it possible to sum up Mr. Gore's books more accurately? He is perfectly willing to over look the manipulation of scientific data in order to make certain decades look cooler and others warmer in order to support the notion of global warming. He calls it 'settled science' although hundreds of scientist have stated that it isn't. His ultimate goal is global energy rationing. He wants to, 'use the rule of law as an instrument of human redemption.' He is trying to influence the passage of an energy rationing bill. He uses his Alliance for Climate Change to convince people that there is a global warming 'crisis'. He is set to become a billionaire by profiting from government policies being enacted because of this non-existent crisis.

"Let us examine this so called 'settled science'? Observe my next character, Michael Mann. Like Dr. Simon Pritchett, he is a professor who earns his livelihood from tax payer money, from public universities and public grants. Dr. Pritchett believes that values don't exist, but are invented. Mr. Mann produced a graph showing a great leap in global warming during the second half of the twentieth century. It was later revealed that the data used to prepare the graph was intentionally distorted. Some astrophysicists believe that most global warming is caused by solar variation, and that the 20th century is not the warmest one of the last millennium. However, that doesn't play into the hands of those that want to cripple your economy, and create a crisis, for their own reasons.

"The graph was used as the basis of a United Nations Report which led to the Kyoto Protocol. The UN is now planning to pass a treaty that restricts America's carbon emissions while allowing China, which has the most emissions of any country in the world, to continue un-effected. The Virginia attorney general is investigating Mr. Mann for possible fraud when he sought grants for global warming research. A speech has been made in the United States Senate stating 'that man-made global warming is the greatest hoax ever perpetrated on the American people.' With these two men you see a direct example of my theme of government employees collaborating for their own benefit and against the best interests of their country."

I must admit that I never cared much for the former vice-president, he always seemed like a phony to me. From his claims to having invented the internet to this global warming thing, nothing about him rings true. His Nobel peace prize for global warming makes about as much sense as President Obama's Nobel peace prize for what he hopes to accomplish. Like his "love story" marriage, this global warming thing could all fall apart in the end.

"These people could never get away with their schemes if it weren't for the deliberate compliance of the news media. It was they that enabled the election of this President, and they who advance his policies. I shall now turn my attention to Mr. Kieth Olbermann. My character, Bertram Scudder, is an angry journalist that writes essays supporting the Statist. Mr. Olberman, having spent the first twenty years of his career as a sports announcer, has somehow become qualified to be the voice of the extreme left. He called the man who was soon to become the Senator from Massachusetts "an irresponsible, homophobic, racist, reactionary" that supported violence against women and politicians that disagreed with him. He had no facts to support any of those statements, and was forced to apologize for them. With no factual evidence, he claims that the Tea Party is a racist organization. He speaks of its 'blind hatred' and 'disinterest in the welfare of others' with no evidence to support his words. He laments 'the narrowness of their minds' like the elitist he is. Are you beginning to see how these people interact with each other in order to accomplish their goals?'

"You talk as if there is a conspiracy by Liberals to take over this country. I don't see how they could possibly succeed if they only represent 20% of the voters"

"I think you will, when I am finished. Perhaps the most outrageous person of all is Mr. Moore. My Balf Eubank character is intended to show how low the arts and culture of this country has sunk. Mr. Moore is the living embodiment of this. His films are propaganda of the worst kind. He has the looter's mentality. He believes it to be a moral imperative to confiscate from the rich and give their wealth to the poor. Once you concede the principle of this action, that stealing property from a person that earned it in order to give it to someone who didn't, is morally correct, you are finished! After that it is only a matter of them deciding who is rich and who is poor. First candidate Obama said that someone earning $250,000 a year was rich, and then he lowered it to $200,000. They will always keep lowering it, until everyone is equally poor, that is their ultimate goal.

"Mr. Moore portrays Cuba's hospitals as the ultimate in health care, never mentioning that the one's he shows are for non-Cubans only. The hospitals the citizens of that country are allowed into are not fit for human habitation, in fact, you wouldn't send your dog to one of them. His heroes are the people who lived beyond their means and then defaulted on their debts. His villains are those whom the government forced to lend them money and then tried to collect on those worthless debts. In his film, 'Capitalism', he states that 'capitalism is an evil and you cannot regulate evil. You have to eliminate it and replace it...' And what does he want to replace it with? 'What I'm asking for is a new economic order... that has an ethical and moral core to it. That nothing is done without considering the ethical nature, no business decision is made without first asking the question, is this for the common good?' He further believes '...that Wall Street and the banks are truly the enemy, and we need to tie that beast down and quick.' Surely you agree that this is almost word for word what the Stastist preach in my novel."

"I've never seen any of his movies, but I've heard about them. He take's a very one sided view of everything, never allowing a contradictory opinion. What I've seen of him on television and his positions that he's stated corresponds to what you said."

"It is difficult to see any heroes in America today. Some people have some of the attributes of a hero, but fall short in many ways. That is why your country is in the situation it now finds itself. So I've chosen two people who have some of the characteristics of my heroes, but not all of them.

"Sarah Palin has suffered all of the vilification and innuendo of the Statist mentality as Dagny Taggert, for most of the same reasons. She managed the largest state in the union, Dagny managed the largest railroad. She generally speaks rationally, stating facts, as opposed to the obfustication of most politicians. She is pro-industrial while her critics are anti-industrial. She wanted to develop the natural resources of Alaska, the Statist opposed her every step of the way.

"As a mayor she reduced property taxes by 75% and eliminated personal property and business inventory taxes. She set as her goals resources, work force and infrastructure development. She was a champion of ethics reform. She told the people of Alaska that they had to develop their own economy, because they should not rely on federal government spending, at a time when her state was the largest per-capita recipient of federal earmarks. She later signed a bill authorizing the construction of a natural gas line from Alaska's North Slope to the Continental United States.

"Like Dagney, she has had to fight the Statist all of her working life. Being unable to attack her for her views, they attack her and her family in the most vicious personal way. I consider her a hero because she generally opposes the Statist in favor of the producers and those who believe in self sufficiency. Her motivation is religious, mine is not. This leads to several issues that we do not agree on. But Dagney also had errors in her reasoning; they did not prevent her from being a hero. Her motivations, like Dagney's, are the correct ones."

I'm not certain where I stand with Mrs. Palin. I like what she says, but I don't think she is ready to be President. We now have a person who had no qualifications to be President leading this county, and we are in a terrible mess. I don't think we can afford to try to train another one on the job. We need somebody who has the proven ability to take control of our government and tame it. She might prove herself able to do it in the future, but I'm not convinced that she is ready now.

"Steve Jobs' story is much like Hank Rearden's. He is a man who advises people not to live with the results of other people's thinking. His stated belief is that 'innovation distinguishes between a leader and a follower.' Like Rearden, he is not college educated and is a self made man that loves his work. He is the founder of three companies. He turned an enterprise that he helped start in his garage into a multi-billion dollar company with thousands of employees. His career and spirit are very much like Hank Rearden's, as are his errors.

"President Obama is like Mr. Thompson in many ways. Neither merits a first name that is well known, which is symbolic of how little is known about them. He is a product of the looter's system of Chicago and is indecisive, unable to think outside of that system. He was a state senator from 1997 through 2004, and was elected a U.S. Senator in 2005 and almost immediately began his campaign for President. These are the 'qualifications' of the man holding the most important job in the world. I shall have more to say about him later.

"There are some minor characters represented too. Andrew Stern, SEIU leader, represents Fred Kinnan, the corrupt union leader. Mr. Stern has been the most frequent visitor to the White House. His union's PAC contributed more than $27 million to Mr. Obama's Presidential campaign. Cindy Sheehan, the activist, is the personification of Kip's Mom, a woman who uses her son's death to promote her political agenda. You might also be interested in knowing that John Galt's motor is represented by the science of cold fusion, which has the potential of providing unlimited, inexpensive clean energy if pursued to conclusion."

"All right, I'll concede that there are some actual people that resemble your characters, but what has that got to do with the condition our country is in today?"

"America is in decline because the type of government policies that I predicted would be put in place in my story are a reality today. The Emergency Economic Stabilization Act of 2008, which your conservative President rushed to sign just hours after congress passed it, is exactly what I foretold. In its aftermath the government ended up owning 61 percent of General Motors' stock. They then went on to bail out Chrysler and ruin their bond holders in favor of the auto union. This is precisely the sort of government 'preferential treatment' business dealing that takes place throughout my book, with no recourse to the victim allowed."

Everything she said was true, but I still didn't see how a lot of isolated government issues constituted a pattern, or "theme." It was generally understood by anyone that paid the slightest attention to the Presidential campaign that Obama was going to govern from the left, that's what the people voted for. I didn't see any grand design behind all of those events; it was just politics as usual. I was used to it, the candidates that I voted for rarely won.

"You've pointed out a few isolated instances of the government pushing its weight around, but that's not proof that it's trying to turn us into the decaying socialist America that you portray in your book"

"I shall now present that proof to you. I will illustrate how a plan conceived by two university professors in the 1960's has been systematically enacted to elect a 'progressive' President and congress with the specific intention of turning America into a Socialist country and the means they are using to accomplish their goal."

That got my attention! A 50 year old plan that resulted in the election of a president and congress that wanted to Socialize America. That was hard to believe.

"It is called the Cloward-Piven strategy. Its goal is to destroy Capitalism by creating an overwhelming demand for government services, one that would be impossible to fulfill, and therefore cause a crisis and economic collapse. Their method is to make society afraid of poor people. Their intent is to destroy the welfare system in order to create a political and financial crises. They believed that the poor people will then revolt and demand a welfare state. The method that they have adopted to achieve these goals was one put forward by Saul Alinsky.

"Mr. Alinsky believed in the Trojan horse theory of revolution favored by Lenin and Stalin. He wanted to penetrate existing institutions such as churches, unions and political parties, and introduce gradual changes from within them. This is a man who placed 'human rights' far above property rights, as if there could be any human rights without property rights. Hillary Clinton wrote her senior thesis about Saul Alinsky. She said... 'I argued that Alinsky was right...'

"George Wiley was chosen to lead their movement. In 1967 he founded the National Welfare Rights Organization. In 1969 they had 523 chapters. It conducted mass demonstrations of welfare recipients, school boycotts, and other protests. In nine years the number of households on welfare rose 251%, during good economic times. In your city in the 1970's one person was on welfare for every two working in the private economy. This forced New York to declare bankruptcy in 1975. This was a direct result and goal of the Cloward-Piven strategy to destroy the welfare system. The backlash led to the so-called 'end of welfare as we know it' bill signed by President Clinton as Mr. Cloward and Miss Piven looked on.

"Having succeeded in their goal of overwhelming the welfare system, they devised a new strategy, a voting rights movement. This was led by veterans of the welfare rights crusade. They created the organizations Project Vote, an ACORN front, and Human SERVE.

These lobbied for the 'motor-voter' law, also signed by President Clinton with Mr. Cloward and Miss Piven in attendance. The result of that law was massive voter fraud. They were able to overwhelm the nation's electoral system, which eventually led to the Florida recount crisis of 2000. This was another success in their campaign to destroy America's institutions. Remember, these people's main goal is to create crises.

"This brings me to ACORN. This is what the staff report of the 111th Congress has to say about that organization. 'They have repeatedly and deliberately engaged in systemic fraud. Since 1994 more than $53 million in federal funds have been pumped into ACORN, and under the Obama administration, ACORN stands to receive a whopping $8.5 billion in available stimulus funds.' Senator Obama's presidential campaign paid more than $800,000 to an offshoot of ACORN, Citizens Services, Inc., which ACORN described as its 'campaign services entity.' Keith Olberman was one of its most outspoken defenders during the 2008 Presidential campaign. He is employed by a network who's CEO is Jeffrey Immelt. George Soros contributed millions of dollars to it through various organizations, including movon.org. That organization supported Michel Moore's movies, and he supported them. Andrew Stern's SEIU has given it more than $6 million in the last four years.

"So these people, who represent my characters in 'Atlas Shrugged', are all connected to ACORN, and through it played a major role in getting Mr. Obama elected. Let us now look at the history of this organization and his affiliation with it.

"The Presidnt's first mentor was Frank Davis, a Communist. Mr. Obama started the Developing Communities Project based upon the organizing traditions of Saul Alinsky. In 1992 he directed Illinois' Project Vote, the organization with ties to Cloward-Piven. Wade Rathke, Bill Ayres and George Wiley, all members of the radical Students for a Democratic Society, were also involved with it. Mr. Obama was introduced to Mr. Ayres by Alice Palmer, who had been an official of the U.S. Peace Council, a Communist front group. Mr. Rathke is the co-founder of ACORN and SEIU local 100 and worked for the National Welfare Right Organization in Massachusetts. SEIU was headed by Andrew Stern, whom President Obama recently appointed to serve on his deficit commission. Mr. Wiley founded the NWRO. In 1995, with the support of Bill Ayres, Mr. Obama became the first chairman of the Chicago Annenberg Challenge, which gave $175,000 to Michael Klonsky, who founded what became the Communist Party (Marxist-Leninist). He later became a member of the board of the Woods Fund of Chicago, along with Mr. Ayres, which contributed substantially to ACORN. In 2006 Mr. Obama supported the interests of ACORN 100%. Everywhere you look, his trail leads back to ACORN and its radical founders."

"So you're saying that the President has always been a member of the radical left and had been propelled into the presidency by them?"

"Exactly! They developed their most recent tactics and built up their organizations during the 2004 election, and brought them to fruition in 2008."

This was more than I could accept. She was talking about a revolution imposed upon the government by itself. Why?

"You claim that they are trying to change our economic system from Capitalism to Socialism, but why would they want to do that?"

"There is only one answer to that question, power. The power to impose their will upon the people, to make you live the lives that they think you should lead, with them writing and enforcing the laws to make you do it. The true believers will contribute hundreds of millions of dollars of their personal fortunes to achieve their goals. Consider this, the Democrats have had about 60 years of controlling congress, and in that time we have gone from one crisis to another. Why? Are they that stupid or do they continue to pass disastrous laws because they somehow benefit from doing so, as in 'Atlas Shrugged'?

"Look at their recent record. The health care bill made 30 million more people dependent on government assistance and added trillions to the national debt. They refuse to secure your borders, allowing millions of illegal immigrants into this country. These are overwhelmingly people that will require government services, and help to overload the system. Cap and trade will provides even more government control of the economy. That plus healthcare will add hundreds of thousands of people to the government payroll. They obstructed the clean up of the Gulf oil spill, using 'environmental issues' as an excuse, changing it from a potential hazard into an economic and environmental disaster. They passed laws requiring banks to make 'sub-prime' mortgages, which resulted in bank failures, which resulted in government bailouts, which resulted in the economic collapse that they blamed on 'big business'. They create crisis after crisis and then proclaim, as Mrs. Clinton and Rahm Emanuel did, 'never let a good crisis go to waste.' What you are witnessing is the Cloward-Piven strategy being enacted at the highest levels of government."

It's true, I thought, it all added up. How did it come to this? Were we too consumed with our personal lives to pay attention? Did we give the politicians too much power and not enough supervision? Worst of all, did we all just want to believe that we could keep on receiving entitlements without ever having to pay the price for them. I realized that I was as guilty as anyone else in allowing it to happen. But what could be done now?

"There is still one of your characters that you haven't mentioned."

"Yes, of course I'm aware of that, I wanted to be sure that you understood the situation first."

"Who is John Galt?"

"You are! You, and all of the people going to the town hall meetings, tea party rallies and other protests against this administration's attempt to socialize this country. John Galt defeats the Statist by uniting the thinking, reasoning people of this country to destroy them. November 2010 may well be your last chance to do this. If you do not flush them from your government then, you might never do it."

"There are some major problems in doing that. More than 75% of Americans consider themselves to be Christians, and therefore 'their brother's keeper.' They want to help those less fortunate than themselves. They support most of the social programs."

"Then let them do it the way Americans have always done it, through their own voluntary contributions that they can afford to make. If this is what makes them happy, I have no objection to it. It is the forced taking of wealth from people that earned it to redistribute to those that haven't that I oppose. There is no reason the other 25% should be made to be their brother's keeper if they do not believe that it is their obligation."

"There is no way that we are going to eliminate all of the social programs that are now in place. The largest generation in our history is about to retire and depend on Social Security and Medicare for much of their livelihood. They paid into these programs all of their working lives and have earned their benefits."

"What they paid were taxes disguised as insurance payments. That money went into the treasury and was spent like all other taxes. The government then wrote itself I.O.U.'s for it. That makes as much sense as you writing one to yourself, and does as much good. These programs should gradually be phased out, and then eliminated. The amount of money, adjusted for inflation, each individual had forcibly taken from them should be calculated, and then returned to them with an appropriate amount of interest. That is how much they have earned, any amount above that was confiscated from someone else. No new contributions should be made, let the people that earned the money decide how to invest it. If they choose not to, it is their choice and they must be made to bear the consequences of their decisions, not the public."

"I don't know if that is possible. There is one thing I have never understood about American society. The very liberal left is only about 20% of the public, and they are mostly non-Christian or atheists, but they are the ones pushing for more and more social programs. On the other hand, the Christians tend to be conservative, and oppose these programs even though they correspond to their religious beliefs. Each group takes the opposite position that you would expect them to. How do you explain this contradiction?"

"There are no contradictions in the natural universe, what is, is! When you encounter what appears to be one, you must examine your premises. Since the liberals are not doing it for religious reasons, they must have some other motive, which I told you was to create crises. They have no concern for the people receiving those benefits, they only see them as voting blocks. The Christians oppose the programs because they instinctively know that their beliefs are being used against them, that they will be drained of everything they produce and own in order to feed the infinite appetite of their so called 'brothers', that in the end they will all be equally devastated. They know it instinctively, but not intellectually. If they examine the facts in a rational manner, the contradiction will ceases to exist.

"As I stated earlier, the liberals are elitists. They believe that the general population is too ignorant to take care of itself and must be forced to do it by regulations that they impose upon them. In their view of the best of all possible worlds, they rule absolutely, as do the dictators in China, Cuba and North Korea. If they achieve their ambitions, this country will eventually look like those countries. This is your choice, look forward to a free and prosperous America, where every citizen succeeds according to his ability, or backward to a country where each succeeds according to his need, at the expense of those with ability. That is what you will be voting for in November. The information you require is at your finger tips, on the internet. Look at your representative's voting records and vote the big government Statist out. As you noted, NOW is the time for all good men, and women, to come to the aid of their country!"

Earth vs. the mole people from the planet formerly known as Siliconia

"Madam President, it's here," the anguished aide said.

"Put it in the TV," the President responded with authority. The aide took the disc that had just been received from SETI and placed it into the DVD player. The fully assembled Presidential cabinet and their advisors watched him nervously. This was the first crisis of the new administration. "Review the situation for the full cabinet," the President told the aide.

"Yes. Well, SETI began receiving these transmissions last night. They were sent as ordinary television signals, in full color high def with surround sound. At first they thought it was some kind of a prank, and it took them a while to confirm that they were actually coming from outer space. They estimated they were originally sent from about a light year away. But the thing is, they're moving closer all the time. That's when they notified the government."

"Give me the remote." the President said. She turned on the DVD player.

"Greetings, people of Earth!" a voice said. The screen was blank. "We are the last surviving Siliconians. We have been monitoring your television signals for the past fifty years and have learned eighty four of your languages. We have chosen English to communicate with you since it was the one most frequently used in your broadcasts. I would like to explain who we are and why we are coming to settle on your planet before broadcasting pictures of ourselves, in order to minimize the cultural shock to you."

The President stopped the recording. "Why do they sound so condescending, like they're talking to children?" she said. The assembled cabinet looked at each other and shrugged, their faces were blank. "Are there any laws that require us to accept them?" she asked her Attorney General.

"Well, they call themselves survivors. On the high seas we would be obligated to render assistance to any survivors we encountered. But I'm not sure those laws would apply to outer space. I don't believe that they would have any legal claims to settle here."

"Good, that ought to give them some cultural shock." She pressed the 'play' button.

"Our former home, the tiny planet we called Siliconia, no longer exists. It was made up entirely of sand. We thrived there, building large cities and developing a sophisticated culture. Sand was the source of our food, energy, and building materials. We lived there happily for tens of thousands of years before anybody noticed that our planet was shrinking. Our scientist tried to warn the general population about what was happening, but they wouldn't listen. Even as Siliconia was disappearing beneath our feet, they were helpless to stop the mindless consumption of it. A few of us realized that our planet was doomed, so we built a small fleet of spaceships. Unfortunately, these had to be fueled with sand. By the time they were ready, there wasn't much left of our planet. When we launched, what was left of it was sucked into our fuel tanks, and our planet just disappeared. It was very sad."

The President stopped the recording again. "This is some kind of a bad joke," she said. "It's those 'anti-greens' trying to make us look bad. Where's our Green Giant? Al?"

"Over here, Madam President"

"Al, you're the 'King of Green', what do you make of this?"

"Well, it sounds a lot like our global warming problem, only it got completely out of control. We could use it to scare the daylights out of the people. It would really shut those anti-greens up once and for all."

"Good point Al. Let's hear what else they have to say." She pushed 'play'.

"We do not come as beggars; we have a lot to offer you. You have limitless deserts that contain more sand than our tiny planet ever had. We can show you how to convert it into inexpensive clean energy, enabling you to reduce or even eliminate your need for fossil fuels. The residue is stronger than steel, and non-corrosive. You could build structures that reached into your atmosphere with it. It lasts forever."

"We have a problem Madam President," the Union's multimillionaire representative of the working people said. She stopped the recording.

"What is it John? By the way, nice haircut."

"Thanks. All that cheap energy is going to cause havoc in the oil markets and crisis in the Middle East. Those buildings that last forever are going to cost our people thousands of jobs. Our economy will be a mess. We'll never get re-elected."

"Yes, we may have to restrain the use of some of their technology, for the good of the people." She pressed the 'play' button.

"Now that you have had an opportunity to listen to us, and know that we mean you no harm, I believe it is safe to reveal our features to you. I am starting the video transmission now."

A picture appeared on the screen and a loud gasp went up from the room. The president froze the picture on the large screen. "They look like moles!" someone said. "Oh, my God!" cried another. Other comments were: "This is a disaster!"; "Look at their skin, it's a furry brown!"; "They're naked!"

For some reason the President thought of her husband, she fought off a feeling of nausea. . "Pull your selves together," she said, "We've all seen worse things than this before." She resumed the recording.

"We will soon be within range to establish two way communications with you. We are traveling at what you call 'warp five' speed, and should be able to do so in a few days. Until then, we wish you well."

"What the hell is 'warp five?" the President said. "Where's our 'space and feelings' advisor?"

"She monitoring this in the outer office, I had her standing by just in case." the aide said. "Send Whoopee in!" he shouted into the intercom.

She came into the meeting room. "Why are you wearing that funny hat?" the President asked her.

"Well, all that I was told was that this meeting had something to do with space, and I just felt…."

"Never mind," the President interrupted, "do you know what 'warp five' means?"

"Oh, sure. That's five times the speed of light. When Captain Picard was in a hurry…."

"Skip the details. I thought it was impossible to go faster than the speed of light. What else can you tell me?"

"Well, there was this thing called the 'Prime Directive' that he was always breaking…."

"What does that have to do with anything?"

"Well, if they know about warp drive, they might also know about that, and I feel that it could cause you some problems. They might expect you to do some things that you don't want to do."

"All right, let's move on…."

"They're in the outer office too, I'll call them," said aide. He spoke into the intercom.

"No, I meant… Oh, what the hell, might as well have them in here too. I owe them."

A man and woman came into the meeting room. She greeted them by name, "Hello, Mr. Moov, Ms. Ahn, nice to see you again. You can just listen in for background information in case we need to involve you later."

"This looks important", the man said. "Where's the Veep?

"Oh, he's still mad about you calling him the whitest black man since Al Jolson. He won't come to any of our meetings."

"Yeah, that was sweet. It took all of the air out of his balloon and handed you the nomination. It was classic. It's why you're the Pres and he's not."

"A lot of people thought it was a cheap shot."

"You don't get it, do you? Everything is perception. A woman goes to the market and buys an apple because it looks good. She gets it home and it tastes like crap so she throws it in the garbage. Next week she does it all over again. The only way to stop her from buying the apple is to make it look rotten. That's our job. Appearances are everything. Destroy a person's appearance and you destroy him. You owe us big time. That reminds me, George wants to know when you're going to invite him to the white house for a sleepover. He says you owe him."

"Tell him thanks and we're working on it," the President said. "God, is there anybody in the world that we don't owe?" she thought.

"Who the hell is Al Jolson anyway?" somebody asked.

"Was," Whoopee answered. "He's been dead a long time. He was a white singer in the thirties who put black grease paint on his hands and face and sang about his 'Mammy'. He made the first talking picture, 'The Jazz Singer'. Whitey ate it up, the black folks hated it."

"So, who remembers him now?"

"The older black people, and they're the ones that vote, or didn't vote, after that smear."

"You're much too sensitive Whoopee, all's fair in love and politics." Ms. Ahn said.

"Just remember, I'm the one that went into the lion's den and took on O'Rilley. Nobody in this room dared to do it. I fought him to a draw; he had to admit that my feelings were as valid as his facts about Iraq."

"I know, I know, you didn't get your job here because of your space expertise."

"Can we move… continue the discussion?" the President asked. "Whoopee, what are your feelings about the situation?"

"We have to look at the big picture. These are brown skinned illegal aliens who have lost their homes and are coming here to find a better life. They have much to offer us and ask little in return. We have to welcome them with open arms, that's always been our party's policy."

"Oh my God!" someone moaned.

The President turned pale. She wondered how much it was going to cost to settle these mole people and what political price she would have to pay. "There must be some logical way to examine this situation based on principles and facts," she said.

"We're secular-progressive liberals, we don't use logic or facts, and don't have any principles," Al responded.

For a moment the President considered having him shot, but decided against it. She called on her Secretary of Defense. "What do you have to say about all of this, Doctor Nukem?"

"It's Doctor Newcome, Madam President."

"Oh yes, of course. You were a professor of economics at Colombia, weren't you?"

"Yes, as everyone knows, wars are all about economics, that's why you chose me. Also you owed Colombia big time."

"So, what is your read on the situation?"

"Well, I tend to agree with John, too much cheap energy would destroy our economy. Why would anyone want to work? As for structures that lasted forever, that would ruin our building industry. If you use this material to build cars, then you'll have cars that last forever and run on cheap energy, a major disaster. These mole people cannot be allowed to devastate us that way. We must destroy them."

"Isn't that a bit harsh? What would history say about me if we killed the first visitors from another planet? It would set a terrible precedent."

"Don't worry about history, no one will remember them, after all, who remembers the Kickapoo Indians?"

"Who?"

"See what I mean?"

"I guess so." She wondered what Bill would do. Of course, take a poll! Nobody can blame me if things get screwed up because I did what the people wanted. "I think we might want to get some polling data on this question before we make any decisions," she said. There were murmurs of agreement. "Great idea!" someone said. The President turned to her aide and told him to arrange the poll.

"No problem, how do we want it to come out?" he asked.

"What do you mean?"

"Do we want the results to have them stay or leave? We have to know how to phrase the question to get the results we want. We could phrase it, 'The aliens offer us unlimited clean energy in exchange for our useless deserts, should we accept their offer and let them stay?' That would get us a yes vote, or we could word it, 'These rodent people want to worm their way into our pristine deserts and destroy our economy with their gadgets, should we let them?' if we want a no vote."

"Can't we just ask a neutral question and get an accurate response?" the President inquired.

"A neutral question? Never thought of that. Very unusual for a political poll. I suppose someone could think of one, but it might take some time."

"Work on it." the President sighed.

*   *   *   *   *   *   *   *   *   *   *   *

"It's coming in now, Madam President. They asked to talk to you." The aide said.

She looked around the room at her re-assembled cabinet and advisors and said, "All right, this is it. Let's be professional about this. The whole world is watching and this is live, so we can't edit anything. Turn on the monitors and cameras."

A technician from the television pool threw a switch and the giant television screen in the front of the room came to life. The face of a mole person appeared, and she again felt that nausea that overwhelmed her the first time she saw it..

"Good day, Madam President, allow me to introduce myself. You may refer to me as Mosses. That is not my Siliconian name, of course, which is 'Scrtlaeex', un- pronounceable by you. I have chosen an Earth name to facilitate communications between us. Your Mosses was a man who led his people through the wilderness for many years, to a new world, as am I. In fact, all of us have taken American names that we learned from your television shows."

The President was momentarily stunned. He was playing the 'religion' card. She recovered quickly. "Greetings, Mr. Mosses, I am honored to meet with such a remarkable being. May I offer our condolences for the loss of you planet?"

"Thank you. I am aware that our appearance may be a bit unsettling to you, as yours is to us, but we do have our commonalities. We are all mammals, for instance."

She looked around the room for her science advisor and made eye contact with her. Alicia stood up and nodded her head up and down to the President in conformation. All the men in the room, and some of the women, visualized her swimming naked in her pool.

"Yes, that is quite comforting, sort of like whales, which everyone love." That will put them in their place, she thought.

"Exactly, except that we are more technology advanced."

"Damn, he got me that time," the President thought; "he implied that they were more advanced than we were."

"Yes, your space technology is most impressive; do you have nuclear energy as well?"

"No, we never fought amongst ourselves, so we never had the need to create weapons of any kind. Silicon is our only energy source, and we have very little of it left."

"Yes!" The President thought. Her cabinet gave her the 'thumbs up' sign. "What is it that you request of us, Mr. Mosses?" she asked.

"We have seen from your films, 'Lawrence of Arabia' is my favorite, that you have vast deserts of unused sand. We merely wish to settle there and co-exist peacefully with you. Arizona, Nevada and New Mexico will do very nicely. Of course, the Sahara and Gobi desserts are also quite acceptable."

"How many of you are there?" The President inquired.

"We have five ships, each containing fifty three of our people."

"We will need some time to consider your request. The deserts that you mentioned are in various countries, and they will have to be consulted. Please contact us again in three days."

"Yes, I understand. Good day, Madam President."

The President turned off the television set. "Well Joe, what's the UN going to make of this?" she asked the ambassador to the United Nations.

"We have a major problem. The Sahara covers twelve countries, and we'll never get them to agree to anything. The Gobi is in China, and is not really a 'sand' dessert. That leaves three of our states as only possible location for them. They're going to expect us to take them in anyway. You know, it's that 'give me your tired, your poor, your huddled masses yearning to breath free' thing."

"You mean from the Statue of Liberty?"

"Oh, is that where it's from? Well, yes, that's what I mean."

"So we're stuck with them?" she asked. There were murmurs of agreement.

"Bill, what are your people in New Mexico going to think about their new mole neighbors"

The former senator stood up immediately. "Let me make it perfectly clear to you, Madam President, they are not going to want them in their back yards. In my state we kill moles when they invade our property. You can be sure that Arizona and Nevada share this view.

"Does anyone have any suggestions?" she pleaded.

"We have to make the poll show that the over whelming majority of Americans don't want them to land here," the aide said.

"I have an idea," Mr. Moov said, "we take get a picture of some young moles, and run it with the caption, 'Do you want these child mole nesters in your back yard?' Get it?"

"But moles don't build nests," someone said.

"What's that got to do with anything?"

"I have to admit, you guys are really good at what you do," the President said grudgingly. .

"Nobody does it better…" Ms. Ahn started to sing.

"Wait!" Whoopee shouted. "You can't do this. It's against everything we said we believed in."

"I told you," Al said, "we don't believe in anything, except votes of course, and moles can't vote." There were more murmurs of agreement.

"Let me see a show of hands for the poll." The President said. Everyone in the room except Whoopee raised their hands. "All right, it's unanimous, democracy has been served. Take the poll, and make sure it comes back overwhelmingly negative."

"I'm out of here!" Whoopee said. "You'll find my resignation on your desk in the morning." She stormed out of the room.

"She is much too sensitive for politics." Al said. "Who can we get to replace her?"

"What about Jessie or Al?" someone suggested.

"No, they're too independent and too soft." Ms. Ahn replied. "I know just the man. Do you remember the black guy that called the black Fox news caster a 'happy Negro' on CNN? That's the kind of guts we need. I think we can lure him away from Syracuse University."

"That's would offend a lot of our black constituents," the President said.

"It'll keep the 'Uncle Toms' in their place, and allow the activist to roam free. That's what we want, isn't it?"

"Well, if you think it's a good idea, look into it." You can't reason with these people,she thought. They reminded her of the attack dogs in "Animal Farm".

*   *   *   *   *   *   *   *   *   *   *   *

After terminating his communication with the President, Mr. Mosses held a conference call with the captains of the other space crafts. Since they were all taking immersion classes in English that was the language that they spoke.

"Has everyone listened to the voice transmissions from the President's meeting room?" Mr. Mosses asked. Their technology, unknown to the President, had allowed them to attach an audio tracer signal to their television signal and pick up conversations in the Presidents meeting room after the television conference was completed. This had been transmitted to them. "Child mole nesters indeed!"

"It appears that we've made a tactical error," Captain Riker said. "We placed too much emphasis on shows like 'Leave it to Beaver' and 'Father knows best'. We assumed that these were typical of human behavior. Obviously we were misguided."

"I agree." said Captain Worf. It is quite clear now that 'Dr. Strangelove' is more typical of their behavior. We must adjust our plans. We may have to force ourselves upon them. We are almost out of fuel."

"But their prime directive decrees that we be treated as one of them," Captain Picard interjected.

"I don't think that they take it very seriously," Mr. Mosses said. "In fact, I'm not even sure they can travel at warp speed. They seem very different than the people we saw in their television broadcasts. Did you notice that there wasn't always laughter after somebody said something? I agree that we've been mislead by those broadcasts."

"And they wear clothing all the time," Captain Troy said. "In the movies we saw they were always hurrying to take them off. I sense that something very strange is going on, we should be very careful in our dealings with them."

"Then we agree," Mr. Mosses said. "Go to plan B immediately."

*   *   *   *   *   *   *   *   *   *   *   *

"The results of the poll are in, Madam President," the aide said.

"Are we ahead?"

"I'm talking about the mole poll."

"Oh yes, of course. How did it come out?"

"Exactly the way we planned. Eighty two percent against, eight percent for, and ten percent don't know anything about mole people."

"Wonderful, the people have spoken, what do we do now?"

"Deny them landing rights, which is our privilege under international law. Tell them that if they attempt to land they will be destroyed."

"Isn't that a little harsh; couldn't we let them land long enough to refuel, and then send them on their way? God knows we have enough sand to spare."

"You know how it is with illegal aliens, once they get here, they never want to leave. It'll be a hell of a lot harder to get rid of them once they're in our country."

"I suppose you're right, but it just doesn't seem like the kind of thing our party should be doing."

"Think of them as Republicans."

"Tell the military to go on alert, I don't want any surprises. They say that they don't have any weapons, but can we believe them? After all, they are Repub…moles."

As the small band of survivors from Siliconia approached Earth's atmosphere, they made their final preparations. Mr. Mosses sent his orders to all of the ships. "Set burrowing beam depth to three thousand feet, set burrowing coordinates to pre-determined patterns. We are about to enter Earth's atmosphere. At my mark, turn on your cloaking devices: three; two; one; mark."

*   *   *   *   *   *   *   *   *   *   *

"We have them in our sights, Madam President." The general said into the telephone.

"Are you sure they received our warnings that we would destroy them if they tried to land?"

"Yes, we sent them non-stop for the last two days."

"And the whole world is aware of this?"

"Yes, of course, that was our top priority."

"Then I have a clear conscious, shoot them down."

The General didn't like what he had to do, but orders were orders, especially when they came from the Commander in Chief. Also, he was next in line to head the Joint Chiefs.

"I knew this 'star wars' stuff would come in handy one day" he thought. He hung up the telephone.

"Enter target coordinates into the computers as they appear," he ordered.

"Target coordinates entered sir," a Captain replied.

"Prepare to launch missiles on my order," the general said.

"Missiles ready sir! Damn!"

"What's the matter?"

"We've lost them. They've completely disappeared."

"That's impossible!"

"Come see for yourself."

The general went over to the monitor and saw his target's signals disappear as they entered the earth's atmosphere. "Damn sneaky mole bastards!" he said. "Enter their trajectories into the computer and project a landing area." The Captain did so. "They landed in the middle of the Arizona dessert, hundreds of miles from any occupied areas," he told the general.

"Excellent!" the general replied. "That was a big mistake on their part. It makes it too easy for us."

"Easy for what?"

"Nukes, of course. Get me the White House on the phone again."

The President addressed her assembled cabinet. "Through some treachery on the mole's part we were unable to shoot them down," she said. "I can see now that this was all some vast Siliconian conspiracy to undermine my administration. The commander on the scene is requesting permission to order a nuclear strike. He assures me that there will be no collateral damage. What do you think, Dr. Newcome?"

"Nuke 'em"

"I thought you said it was pronounced 'Newcome"

"It is, that's what you should do, nuke 'em."

"Oh, I see. Does anyone object? Let me see a show of hands." Nobody raised their hand.

"Then it's unanimous. In order to preserve the peace, prosperity and tranquility of our nation, we must obliterate the mole bastards. I'll give the order immediately."

*   *   *   *   *   *   *   *   *   *

Three thousand feet beneath the Arizona desert Mr. Mosses held the most important meeting of his life. "Is everything ready?" he asked his chief scientist.

"Yes, all we need now is someway to 'prime the pump'. We don't have enough energy left to do it on our own."

"Yes, that is the purpose of plan B."

"After that happens, the sand above will be transformed into an impenetrable shield that can withstand anything they have to use against us. It will also start our generators, giving us the energy that we need to be self sufficient."

"What are our prospects on this planet?"

"Given our high birth rate, and their relatively low one, our population should exceed theirs in a few thousand years."

"Yes," Mr. Mosses agreed. "Can you believe that they actually kill their young as a matter of convenience? Most uncivilized!"

"At that time we will be able to surface and take control of the planet. Of course, it is possible that they will destroy themselves before that, in which case we would be able to emerge sooner. In the mean time we will be quite comfortable down here, once the pump is primed, of course."

"Our listening post assures me that the event is eminent. Are we fully prepared?"

"Yes, everything is ready."

Mr. Mosses went to his control panel and spoke to the listening post. "What is their status?" he asked.

"Their airplane took off about twenty minutes ago and should be over head soon. Yes, I have it on my monitor now. It is releasing its weapon. Prepare for impact!"

A rumbling sensation was felt throughout the newly burrowed cavern. The chief scientist went over to his control panel and called out its readings. "The pump is primed, the overhead layers of sand are fused, ample energy is being fed into our generators to start our converters. We are completely self sufficient now. Congratulations, Mr. Mosses!"

"Thank you. Spread the word, we are home!"

Cyber Money

D.J. Average sat at the desk in his small apartment contemplating his next move. Running for President was a little more difficult than he had expected it to be. There had only been eighteen thousand candidates in 2044, a number he could easily have coped with. But this year, 2048, the field had exploded to more than thirty five thousand. These days anyone with an internet connection, which was virtually everyone, could run for President.

He considered his situation. He was a college graduate, with a master's degree in economics, but could only find work for a lousy $40 an hour minimum wage. That came to about $800 a week after taxes and meant flipping hamburgers, or worse, washing dishes. Better to get by on the measly $600 per week unemployment check and stay home. It was outrageous! If you didn't have the connections to get a government job, which half the workforce had, you got a minimum wage job. There was barely anything else in between. The people with connections got the $150 per hour jobs in government, even if they didn't know what they were doing; the unions made sure of that. The members enrolled their children in the union when they were born, so that when they came of age they just stepped into their job. He would be in his late fifties before he was even eligible for one of those jobs, assuming he lived that long. With the nine month waiting list to get into any hospital the slightest illness could kill you. At least he would be able to get decent health care when he became President.

The first problem had been that not everyone running ended up on the official ballot website, which was reserved for the top one thousand candidates. With internet voting from home and the ability to sort the candidates and their positions electronically, thirty five thousand people had been a pretty large field to stand out in. The trick had been to make his name well known enough to be in the top thousand, but not to give away his "big idea" until just before the election, when nobody else could steal it from him. He had danced around it, dropped hints to make them interested, and then hit them with it at the last possible minute. That strategy had worked to get him on the official ballot, now he had to win the election. It was time to make his first posting on the official ballot website.

His first priority was to get the voters attention. The title was extremely important, because that was how the search engines would find it. He typed, "I HAVE THE SOULTION TO OUR COUNTRIES ECONOMIC CRISIS!" He re-read it with satisfaction. Every election for the past fifty years had been about the economy, with every candidate promising to fix it, and every President making it worse. Now the Euro was worth ten dollars, and seventy five percent of the world's trade was in Euros. Social Security and Medicare were almost bankrupt again, despite the fact that the tax had been doubled in the last ten years. Public health care was a shambles, and the dollar was almost worthless outside of the United States. Gold was selling at twenty five hundred dollars an ounce, and oil at seven hundred dollars a barrel. The country was on the verge of economic collapse, and he alone could save it, if he were elected. Then he would get his revenge.

He started typing again. "I am the way, and the light, and those who believe in me shall find eternal prosperity." That should help me with what's left of the religious right, he thought. Now something for the liberals, "With my plan we will be able to raise Social Security and Medicare benefits, Un-employment benefits, Welfare benefits, Universal Health Care benefits, and many more worthwhile government programs at the same time we heal our economy." Those people love to have their cake and eat it too, he reasoned. Next, something for the pro-life, anti-illegal alien people, "My plan will provide Thirty thousand dollars per year, until they are twenty one, to the first three children born of married parents who are legal citizens of the United States. This will eliminate the need for abortions made for financial reasons and encourage illegal aliens to become legal in order to receive these benefits." I have to keep it simple, he reasoned, a little bit of something for everyone. The average attention span is about thirty seconds, the length of a TV commercial or sound bite. After that you loose them. All of those cheap legal mind bending drugs have done their work. And to think that they had dared to mock me! "Go to djaverage.com for more details!" was his final entry.

Davie Jones Average smiled. Revenge would be sweet. Revenge against his parents for giving him a name that made him a laughing stock throughout his school years and wherever he worked (But sweetheart, special names were all the rage when you were born, and your father was an avid stock trader and sailor). Revenge against his teachers for all of the "C+'s" they gave him because his name was "Average", revenge against his employers who never promoted him for the same reason, revenge against the women who shunned him because they couldn't possibly marry a man whose name was "Average" and thus become average themselves. Little did they know that this average man had an I.Q. of 158.

He went to his website to check it yet again. The first thing that appeared was a National Debt Clock. "The National Debt is $35 trillion dollars and is increasing by four billion dollars per day!" a statement above the clock read. I KNOW HOW TO REDUCE BOTH NUMBERS TO ZERO. VOTE FOR ME, D.J. Average, at uspresidentialballot.gov,"

Who ever had the most votes on the first Tuesday in November would be the next President. In three weeks he would make history. After the first week of his posting he had more than seventy thousand hits on his website. People were clamoring to know how he would fulfill his claims. His plan was working beautifully. It was now time to sweeten the pot. He added a new posting. "SOCIAL SECURITY IS NOW TWENTY FIVE TRILLION DOLLARS IN DEBT. I WILL REDUCE THIS TO ZERO AND INCREASE BENEFIT PAYMENTS. VOTE FOR ME, D.J.Average, at: uspresidentialballot.gov.

Ten days before the election he had accumulated more than eight million hits. Even what remained of the print press was writing about his claims. The television commentators voiced skepticism, but since they didn't know what his plan was they couldn't condemn him outright. He logged on to his web site and wrote, "MEDICARE IS EIGHT TRILLION DOLLARS IN DEBT, I WILL REDUCE THIS TO ZERO AND INCREASE THE BENEFITS! Details of my plan will be posted on this web site the Monday before the election. People do love pie in the sky, he thought.

He was the talk of the Internet. The press tried in vain to interview him, but he declined all requests. He never left his apartment. The only thing anyone knew of him was what former co-workers, teachers or friends could remember. On the Monday before the first Tuesday in November he published his plan on his website.

"We are the cyberspace generation," he wrote. "We live, shop, play, make love, and earn our livings in cyberspace. It is only fitting that we should use Cyber Money" He figured that that would grab their flimsy attention. "What is Cyber Money", you ask? It will be the new coin of the realm, I answer. With it we will buy and sell everything on the internet. For example, Social Security beneficiaries will have their payments sent to their computers. They can use it to buy anything on the internet, which is virtually everything. The site that they buy from will use it to pay their tax liabilities, therefore returning it to the government. All internal debts will be converted to Cyber Money. International trade will still be conducted in conventional dollars, so it will not be affected. The value of those dollars will soar once the domestic pressure on them is removed. Ordinary workers paid in paper money will see a tremendous surge in their buying power. It is a win-win situation. Those people dependent on government pensions or welfare will know that their purchasing power is secure and growing, backed by the full faith and credit of the United States government, which has never defaulted on a debt. Productive people will see their taxes reduced and their lifestyle improving. I AM THE ONLY CANDIDATE THAT CAN MAKE THIS HAPPEN! Click here to vote for me, D.J. Average, tomorrow: uspresidentialballot.gov.

The reaction was instantaneous. Millions of people who had not bothered to register to vote went to their computers to do it online. A quick search of their social security number confirmed their eligibility, and they were issued a unique code to use to vote online. On Election Day he received twenty two percent of the vote cast and was elected President.

*   *   *   *   *   *   *   *   *   *   *   *

President Average sat at his desk in the Oval Office and frowned at his financial advisors. They were all older men in their sixties and seventies, not of the cyber generation.

"You cannot issue money with nothing to back it up!" they insisted.

"We've been doing that with paper money since Nixon took us off of the gold standard!" he replied. "President Obama printed money until they ran out of ink."

"They didn't actually print money, they just gave the banks authority to lend money that didn't actually exist accept for numbers in some computers."

"That's what I'm doing, but on a larger scale. Mine doesn't have to be paid back by anyone. "

"His never actually gets paid back either, they just keep rolling it over to future generations who will pay for it with inflated money. He was doing it to stimulate the economy."

"Exactly, that's what I'm doing."

"That was different." They persisted. "That money was backed by the strength of our economy."

"Our economy was a disaster then, and it's a bigger disaster now. Most of it is on the internet these days, which will back up the Cyber Money."

"This is unheard of! You can't just make money out of electronic gigabytes."

"Did you ever hear of AOL, Google or Amazon?" he retorted. "They were pretty good at it. Listen, I'm not asking you, I'm ordering you. I have a mandate from the voters of the United States. Implement it or resign! By the way, all future payments to government employees will be in C.M., so get used to it."

Nobody resigned. On May 26, his birthday, the new currency became legal. All government debt payable to United States citizens was converted to Cyber Money. There was no way to convert "old money", as it came to be known, into C.M., or visa versa. With the enormous burden of public debt removed from it, the value of the old money began to soar. It soon reached par with the Euro. President Average then used it to pay off the huge trade imbalances with the rest of the world. He rejoiced! He had pulled off the greatest Ponzi scheme since the beginning of Social Security, and no one had noticed. When the whole thing falls apart, he would have his revenge.

*　　*　　*　　*　　*　　*　　*　　*　　*　　*　　*　　*

High in the Colorado Mountains, in a very private ski cabin, twenty of the countries most important opinion makers gathered for their annual poker game. Each person brought with them a certified check for one million dollars, with the payable line on it left blank. It was the entry fee for the tournament, at the end of which one player would win the twenty million. Unfortunately, it was only worth a little more that half of what it had been the year before. But money wasn't the main thing that brought them up here, nor was skiing. None of them would have been caught dead on a pair of skis, although the women liked to wear the cute ski outfits. The true purpose of the game was to get them all together to discuss how they would cover important news stories. The poker game was just a cover to keep them from being accused of collusion, which of course was what they were doing.

There were two tables with ten players each. All the owners of the various media sat at the first table, and their star broadcasters, editors and journalists at the second one next to it. It was understood that during the course of the games they would talk about issues that were of concern to most Americans. It was also understood that the table one players would overhear comments from table two and make their opinions known at their table. In this manner they would be conveyed to their subordinates without them telling them specifically what to say or do. Deniability was very important, the journalist had to maintain their integrity.

"What do you think of this CM idea?" the leading network's star anchorman asked no one in particular, as he anted three thousand dollars.

"Craziest thing I ever heard of." Replied a print journalist as he called the bet.

A player at table one picked up on it immediately. "I wouldn't dismiss it out of hand myself," he said. "If the public could be persuaded to accept it, it could be the answer to our problems." Since he was the most powerful person there, everyone hung on his words.

"Yes, but that's a big 'if," The owner of a television network said. "Are the American people that gullible?" He bet fifty thousand dollars.

"There's a classic advertising adage that states, 'nobody ever went broke under-estimating the intelligence of the American public,' an old print reporter said, as he threw in his cards.

"If we pay off our debts and taxes with this CM, then our physical assets will increase in old money value, that helps all of us," a table one player commented.

"But wouldn't that be like what Hitler did, causing run-away inflation of the German currency to pay of Germany's World War One debts?" an anchorwoman asked no body in particular.

"It worked, didn't it?" A table one player said. "Of course, we wouldn't want it to get that far out of hand"

"No, we can control it, after all, we do run the country," the most powerful man there said. This caused some guarded laughter and smiles, and every one concentrated on their card game until the next subject came up. This then, was the manner in which President Average received almost unanimous support for his Cyber money from the independent free press.

*   *   *   *   *   *   *   *   *   *   *   *

Something was wrong, President Average thought. It was now more than a year since the introduction of CM, and there were no signs of economic collapse. By all measures it was stronger than it had been for the last thirty years. The people actually seem to like CM. He read the reports from his economic advisors to find out why.

The first ones to get it had been the Social Security recipients. It had come with a ten percent increase over what they had been receiving. At first they didn't know what to make of it, the report stated, but when they went to the internet to buy groceries that would be delivered to them, and paid for them with CM, they liked the idea. Then they realized that they could buy plane tickets with it, so they could visit their grandchildren. They could also buy presents for them, and book passage on a cruise ship with it. Now they all thought that it was wonderful!

He read the business report. At first big business had resisted CM, but then there had been another baby boom caused by the thirty thousand dollar benefit for the first three children born. The doctors and hospitals were being paid before the mother and child went home. Retail stores were now accepting CM and selling cribs, clothes, diapers and other necessities at a record pace. Computer programs calculated the taxes they owed the various governments and paid them in CM at the time of sale. Business thought it was wonderful!

Another report stated that the homeless people were disappearing from the streets. With access to public internet terminals they were able to collect their increased welfare benefits immediately and use them to rent living space. The building owner's were paid in advance, and used the CM to pay their real estate taxes. All taxes were calculate and automatically paid by government computers, so accountants were no longer needed. It was wonderful!

With the success of CM, The "old money" was gradually withdrawn from circulation by the Treasury department. Everyone was then paid with CM. The illegal immigrants had no access to it, and there was no "Old Money" available to pay them with, so they went back to their home countries. It was wonderful!

*   *   *   *   *   *   *   *   *   *   *   *

Someone, somewhere, is going to have to notice that this whole thing is a house of cards, President Average thought. Some newspaper or TV commentator will surely editorialize on how absurd this whole thing is. When that happens there will be a panic as people race to spend their CM, and the whole thing will collapse. The country will be ruined; and I will have gotten even with all of them. But why hadn't it started yet? He was puzzled.

The one thing he hadn't considered was that the people would love him. President Average's approval rating was over ninety percent. Everybody loved CM, he was a hero. Speeches were made singing his praise; statues of him, heroic, one hand outstretched holding circling electrons to symbolized CM, were placed in town centers. CM was considered the greatest achievement since the creation of the internet.

He sat alone in the Oval office, contemplating the situation; he was not happy. "The best laid plans of mice and men…," he thought. They love me, me! "There are none so blind as those who will not see," the Bible sure got that right. I should have known. The Social Security scam lasted more than a hundred years before people got wise to it, CM will probably do better.

The question was, what should he do about it? Revenge would be sweet, he reflected, but adulation was divine. Re-election was a certainty; after that, back to obscurity, unless…? Unless he could amend the constitution! Why not, it was only a matter of repealing the twenty second amendment. They did it with Prohibition a hundred years ago. The people love me; they should make me President for life! All right, let the fools have their way; let them worship their false god. They will eventually pay the price, meanwhile, I shall rule over them and accept their homage. It is only fitting, I deserve it.

A grateful congress, secure in their elected seats, was only too happy to amend the constitution and make him President for life, the people rejoiced. As the years passed the American economy again became the strongest in the world. The EU issued a version of cyber money, then China followed, and the race was on. In time every country that had access to the internet converted their currency into CM.

The world entered into a Utopian age. There were no wars, as virtually every person in every country had the ability to live quite well on their CM wealth. Trade flowed freely between what had previously been national borders, supported by ample amounts of hard currency that had been freed up by the issuance of CM. Paper money completely disappeared from public use, and by the year 2100 there were very few people who remembered it.

Then one day a twelve year old boy in Indiana was playing in the attic of the house his family had lived in for six generations. He noticed an old trunk he hadn't seen before. He opened it and saw that it was full of old clothes, as he went through them, a strange pair of pants made of a faded blue material caught his eye. He examined it closely, and saw that there was an object in one of its pockets. It was a wallet. It contained some old photos and a green piece of paper with the picture of President Lincoln on it, he recognized the face from his history books. He was an old time President from way before Permanent President Average. There was writing and numbers on the paper: "Five silver dollars payable to the bearer upon demand." There was a date, "1935."; his curiosity was aroused. What was a silver dollar? Who would pay it? What could you do with it? He turned on his wrist comp and accessed the internet. The search for "United States dollar," informed him that congress had set the value of a dollar at 22.23 grains of gold in 1900. So this piece of paper was worth 111 grains of gold. Wow! Further research revealed 480 grains equaled one troy ounce of gold., so this piece of paper was worth about a quarter of an ounce of gold. He wanted it, he could hardly wait until he showed it to the kids at school!

He gave the piece of paper to his father, who had never seen anything like it before. "It says The United States of America on it," he said. "Our bank is called the U.S.C.M.B., which I think stand for United States Cyber Money bank; if we take it there we should be able to get your gold for it."

The next day his father drove him to the bank. The banker, an elderly gentleman, examined the dollar bill carefully. "Yes, I remember this, it was used before CM. Haven't seen one for years. What about it?"

"I want to get the silver dollars so I can exchange them for gold," the boy said.

"Silver? Gold? We don't use that anymore, don't have any here."

"I can't get silver or gold for Cyber money either?"

"No, of course not"

"Then what is it good for?"

"You buy things on the internet with it"

"Can I buy a quarter ounce of gold?"

"No, of course not."

"But it says here on this piece of paper, 'payable upon demand,' his father insisted, "by the United States Government," that's you. That's the basis of CM; if you won't pay this, how do we know you'll pay the CM?"

The banker looked at him and shrugged, "You have to have faith in the government."

The boy and his father went home dejected. They told their friends about the incident, and they in turn told their friends. They had no idea that the "butterfly effect" that they were about to initiate would be the downfall of the world's economy.

Once the question, "What is it good for?" was asked, it could not be retracted. It was repeated over and over again, by thousands of people, then millions, but there was no answer. The "full faith and credit" of the United States government had been breached. People no longer wanted Cyber Money and resorted to bartering. In desperation the Federal bank decreed that Cyber Money could be converted into "old money" at the rate of one cent per C.M., and the "old money" into gold at the rate of $5,000 per ounce. The wealth of America was instantly reduced to one percent of its former value. The wrath of the people turned on President Average. His statues were torn down and he was impeached. The twenty second amendment was re-instated and a new President elected.

D.J. Average was ninety-five years old when his impeachment trial began. He was charged with deliberately destroying the United States economy. He smiled, and pleaded guilty.

Author's note: The following is a script written prior to the 2009 presidential election. It was intended to be used for a Facebook satire, but was never produced.

An Interview with Presidential candidate O'Mama Mia

Voice over: "The following is an exclusive interview by Chris R. Marrow with Presidential candidate O'Mama Mia, presented by NBC, the no-body-cares network.

Chris: "Mr. O'Mama, I can't tell you how excited I am to have you in the studio for this exclusive interview. It actually sends a tingle down my leg."

(Camera shows a small puddle of water near interviewer's leg,, with O'Mama glancing down at it, frowning)

O'Mama: "Um, yes Chris, I'm happy to be here. I'll be pleased to answer any question you might have, but could I first have a glass of water?"

(An attractive female assistant hands him a glass and he thanks her. She swoons to the floor with a smile on her face and is dragged off the set. There is background music of Michel Jackson singing "…ouuuu, I am the one." O'Mama does a little dance to it.)

Chris: "Some people have criticized your lack of experience asking, 'Why did you miss 291 votes in the current session of congress?' and 'What does a community organizer do?' Would you like to reply to them?"

O'Mama: "As you know, the good people of Illinois sent me to the Senate so that I could run for President, which is what I've been doing for the two years since I was elected. This takes a lot of time, so of course I've missed a few votes. What a community organizer does is organize communities! That's no small task on the South Side of Chicago."

(Background music comes up with Frank Sinatra singing "Now the South Side of Chicago is the badest place in town…" O'Mama snaps his fingers to the music).

"Now, some people might think that being the governor of the largest state qualifies you to be President, but that's nothing compared to being a South Side organizer. I mean, you can put lipstick on a moose, but it's still a pig!" (He frowns and taps his left ear.)

Chris: (holding a lit cigarette in his hand) "I'd like to give you the opportunity to straighten out some of the misconceptions that some people may have about you; for instance, during the exhaustive primary season, when you were in several states in one day, you accidentally said that there were only forty seven states. Would you like to correct the record?"

(Chris tosses O'Mama a wiffle ball. O'Mama picks up a plastic bat and hits it past the camera. There is the sound of glass breaking in the background. The camera closes in on O'Mama, smiling.)

O'Mama: "Yes, of course I know there are fifty one states…"
 (There is a pause as O'Mama touches his left ear again, then taps on an earpiece. He talks into a hidden lapel microphone) "…fifty you say! But what about Puerto Rico?" (He touches his left ear again) "Then why did we waste our time campaigning there? We'll have to have them edit this out. Live, what do you mean this interview is live, why didn't you tell me that before? You did? You said it was a 'live' session? I thought you said it was a 'Jive' session.")

Chris anxiously: "Mr. O'Mama?" (he lights another cigarette, holding two in his hand, and inhales on both)

O'Mama; "Let me clarify my last clarification Chris. The people of Puerto Rico were so nice and friendly to me when I was there, that I tend to think of them being a state already, although of course they aren't, but they will be as soon as I become President, you can count on that. We need the extra tax money."

Chris: (holding two lit cigarettes in his hand) "Um, yes. Moving on, there has been some criticism about you being a very shallow person, with no depth. Would you like to respond to that?"

(Chris tosses another wiffle ball to him, he swings and misses.)

O'Mama: "Yes, my opponents have no issues to talk about, so they resort to personal attacks against me. Let me tell you something about me right now, what you see is what you get!"

(Camera shows an Easter basket with jelly beans, etc. with a sign reading "what you see is what you get". Camera, which up until now has only shown upper part of O'Mama's body, pulls back to reveal that he is wearing basketball shorts and tennis shoes under his suit jacket and tie).

"They are going to try to scare you about me! They will say that I have a funny name (pause while he thinks about that statement and frowns), that I don't sound like the people on a dollar bill (another pause), that because I hang out with people who hate America, known terrorists, and convicted felons, I have poor judgment! Well let me say that, that just isn't true, I have the best judgments that money can buy! More than three hundred of them!

Chris: (with three lit cigarettes in his hand) "Um, yes. I'm glad you were able to clarify that, let's move on dot org now. (He pauses nervously, mouthing the words "Did I say that out loud?" His producer nods affirmably). We have a couple from Pennsylvania in the studio that would like to ask you about a statement you made."

 (Camera show a middle aged couple dressed in shabby clothes, with perspiration dripping from their faces. The man is clinging desperately to an air rifle, the woman is clinging to a Bible.)

Man nervously: "Mr. O'Mama, are you going to take away my gun?"

Woman terrified: "Mr. O'Mama, are you going to take away my Bible?"

O'Mama: "No, of course not. I was mis-quoted. What I said is that you were clinging <u>decisively</u> to your guns and Bibles. I admire that. I am a great fan of guns and Bibles, always have been!"

(O'Mama hits a wiffle ball over the couple's head as they cringe in fear.)

Chris: (he wipes perspiration off of his forehead) "Your opponent says that you lack foreign policy experience, citing your statement that Iran is not a threat to us, and then your statement that Iran is a grave threat to us. Would you like to clarify those statements?" (Chris inhales from all three cigarettes, then the camera turns to O'Mama).

O'Mama: "Yes, what I said was that Iran was a tiny country, like Cuba, which is true. But tiny countries can also be a threat. Cuba was a threat during President Kennedy's missile crisis, which he handled so admirably. Of course, that was a defeat for us, like the bay of pigs, but he kept us out of war, which is all that matters."

(O'Mama pulls a wiffle ball out of his pocket, tosses it in the air, and hits it towards Criss. It bounces off of his forehead and he grimaces. He puffs nervously on the three lit cigarettes)

Chris: One last question. You have come under fire for your association with ACORN, which many consider the most radically left organization in this country. Would you like to comment on your work with them?

O'Mama: Yes, the strongest part of my resume, community organizing, was done with this great organization. I am proud of the way that they have helped so many people who couldn't afford to buy a home to buy one anyway, by working closely with Fanny Mae and Freddy Mac."

Chris relieved: "Well, that's all we have time for today. Thank you, and goodnight"

(He inhales deeply from all of the lit cigarettes and then blows a large cloud of smoke at the camera. There is the sound of people coughing as smoke fills the room. Background music comes up with the Platters singing "…you must realize, that when a lovely flame dies, smoke gets in your eyes."

Voiceover: "You've been watching an interview by Chris R. Marrow on (cough) the "no-body-cares" network. (cough, fadeout).

www.ingramcontent.com/pod-product-compliance
Lightning Source LLC
Chambersburg PA
CBHW081539280526
45788CB00010B/3294